THE EVIL STEPMOTHER
VS
SNOW WHITE

The Play

THE EVIL STEPMOTHER VS. SNOW WHITE

The Characters of the Play

Snow White

The Evil Stepmother

Berry O. Blackbird

Prewitt Fox

Sue Lace

Jack Horner

Mr. Wolf

Dwarf Woman

Jack Sprat

Narrator

Skye Blue

King Lee

Bernice, the Fairy Godmother

Judge Thumbelina

Red Riding Hood

Dr. Foster

Willie Ann Winkie

Troll Woman

Boy Blue

Jackie Sprat

Jacque the Camera Man

The Scenes of the Play

Act I   The Commercial

Act II   The Trial

Act III   The Verdict

ACT I

The NARRATOR *stands stage right (or left, whatever).* KING LEE *and* SNOW WHITE *are sitting side by side on two chairs.* KING LEE *is reading a newspaper.*

NARRATOR: Think you know the story of Snow White – the princess with hair as white as snow – no, that's not right. Let me start over. The story of Snow White, the princess whose clothes were as white as snow because - she used a lot of bleach. Wait, that's not it either. Something about her was as white as snow, wasn't it?

SNOW WHITE: My skin! My skin was as white as snow!

NARRATOR: (*turns and says to Snow White*) Oh, right. Anyway, where was I?

SNOW WHITE: White as snow! White as snow!

NARRATOR: Yes, her skin was as white as snow. Everyone knows about the whole poisoned apple and coma thing and the prince waking her up with True Love's Kiss. But there's a lot you don't know. Like that the Evil Stepmother fell off the cliff but she didn't actually die. That was okay until twenty years later when Snow White made a commercial for her business, Poison Proof Apples. Boy, did that ever make the Evil Stepmother angry. I kinda liked the commercial though. Take a look for yourself.

Snow White *stands and performs the commercial.*

SNOW WHITE: (*holds up an apple, as if for a camera and sings as she slowly brings the apple up to her face*) Apple, apple, good for you. Lasts a year, tastes like new.

Full orchestra chimes in (optional, of course. Orchestras are hard to come by, especially since this would be the only piece they play.)

SNOW WHITE: Don't make the same mistake I did and eat an ordinary apple poisoned by your evil stepmother. Buy Poison Proof Apples, grown in the Enchanted Orchard. (*holds apple and smiles*) Potion repellant and oh so tasty too!

KING LEE: Bravo, darling. You're going to sell a lot of apples.

SNOW WHITE: (*sits on her throne beside him*) You think so?

SNOW WHITE*'s cell phone rings, playing 'Someday My Prince Will Come.' She looks around, then starts humming along.*

KING LEE: Your cell phone is ringing.

SNOW WHITE: Oh! (*she pulls a cell phone from a pocket in her dress*) Hello?

SKYE BLUE: (*enters stage left or right, whatever, calling on her cell phone from some place far away.*) Hi, mom, you'll never believe what just happened!

SNOW WHITE: Skye Blue! (*to* KING LEE) Dear, it's Skye Blue.

KING LEE: Ask her how the coach is doing.

SNOW WHITE: Your father said to tell you hi.

KING LEE: Ask her if she's checked the pressure in the coach tires. She has to keep an eye on that.

SNOW WHITE: He wants to know if you've checked the pressure in the coach tires.

KING LEE: What'd she say?

SNOW WHITE: I don't know dear, I just asked her.

SKYE BLUE: I'll check the tire pressure as soon as I get the coach back.

SNOW WHITE: She said she'll do that as soon as she gets the coach back.

KING LEE: (*puts down his paper*) What? What happened to the coach?

SNOW WHITE: I don't know, I wasn't there.

KING LEE: Ask her!

SNOW WHITE: What happened to the coach? Your father wants to know.

SKYE BLUE: Oh, it got stuck in some mud because it was storming and horrible, but the footman said that we were only a mile or so from some castle and if we'd just go down the road, he'd bring our bags directly.

SNOW WHITE: Who's we? Is your brother with you?

SKYE BLUE: I'm using the royal 'we'. I *am* a princess.

KING LEE: What's she saying? What happened to the coach?

SNOW WHITE: (*waives her arm without looking at him*) So what happened?

SKYE BLUE: I got to the castle and they gave me a room here and I got cleaned up. And there's a prince here who's awfully cute, but his mother is really strange. She put me in a room where the bed was so high. There had to have been at least one hundred mattresses.

SNOW WHITE: Mattresses? Is she related to Sleeping Beauty?

KING LEE: She got in an accident with Sleeping Beauty? Isn't she still sleeping?

SKYE BLUE: So I slept on the floor because I was afraid of falling off and I woke up with a sore back. The queen was there when I went down to breakfast and she asked me how I slept and I said not very well and then she said I should marry her son.

SNOW WHITE: What does that have to do with marrying her son?

KING LEE: Sleeping Beauty has a son?

SKYE BLUE: And I just saw your commercial on TV. You sound great, but how's Evil Stepgrandma taking it? Bet she's mad.

SNOW WHITE: Why would she be mad?

KING LEE's *cell phone rings.*

KING LEE: Hello?

PRINCE WILL: *(stage right, or left, whatever, calling from someplace far away)* Hey, dad, I need you to send me an extension ladder by Enchanted Express.

SKYE BLUE: Oh, I gotta go, they're about to give me a tour of the castle.

SNOW WHITE: Don't forget sweetie, watch out for falling giants and let me know what you decide about getting married.

SKYE BLUE: I will. Tell dad I love him too. *(she hangs up and exits.)*

SNOW WHITE: *(notices* KING LEE *is on the phone)* Who is it?

KING LEE: Our son.

SNOW WHITE: Will? Is he alright?

KING LEE: He hasn't said he isn't.

SNOW WHITE: *(loudly)* Son, are you alright?

KING LEE: Stop that, let me talk to the boy. I mean, young man.

SNOW WHITE: They grow up so fast.

PRINCE WILL: Hello? Dad? Can you hear me? (*to the audience*) Why do they talk to each other when I call?

KING LEE: Son, are you still there?

PRINCE WILL: I'm still here.

KING LEE: What do you need an extension ladder for?

SNOW WHITE: Is he stuck on a roof? Again?

PRINCE WILL: I need a ladder because her hair's not growing fast enough.

KING LEE: Her hair?

SNOW WHITE: What's hair got to do with a ladder?

PRINCE WILL: Just send it to The Very Tall Tower.

KING LEE: Do you have any idea what sending something that large by Enchanted Express would cost?

PRINCE WILL: Don't you get a royal discount or something?

KING LEE: I am not sending you a ladder.

PRINCE WILL: How am I going to get her out of that tower then?

KING LEE: I'm sure you'll think of something.

SNOW WHITE: Tell him to look out for falling giants and to clean behind his ears.

KING LEE: She says to tell you she loves you.

PRINCE WILL: Tell her I love her too.

KING LEE: (*gruffly*) And check your tire pressure.

PRINCE WILL: Love you too dad.

They hang up. PRINCE WILL *exits*

SNOW WHITE: I miss our children. Didn't they grow up so fast?

KING LEE: *(pats her hand)* I thought they'd never leave. (*They share a tender look*). Now, tell me what happened to Skye Blue's coach.

SNOW WHITE: Oh, I forgot to tell you, but I got a letter from my Evil Stepmother's attorney.

KING LEE: Your Evil Stepmother? We haven't heard from her in twenty years! What's the letter say?

SNOW WHITE: It says, *(reads from the letter which she pulls out of her pocket)* I am the Evil Stepmother's lawyer. Your commercial is hurting her feelings and it is also against the law. If you do not stop airing this commercial, I am authorized to file suit against you for defamation of character, slander and libel. (*puts the letter back in her pocket*) Do you think it sounds like she's trying to say she's sorry she tried to kill me?

KING LEE: Not exactly. She sounds like she thinks you're lying about something in the commercial.

SNOW WHITE: But the apples *are* potion repellant and oh, so tasty, too.

KING LEE: Maybe it's the part about how she tried to poison you.

SNOW WHITE: Tried? She did poison me. But in the end she did me a favor because we're living happily ever after. Oh, since we're so happy, I hate to make even my Evil Stepmother unhappy. I'm going to send her a coupon for a free bushel of apples. And one to her attorney, too. Even if it doesn't make her happy, at least she'll be healthy. When I saw her last, her complexion was horrible. (*She pats her own pale skin*)

KING LEE: Darling, all this talk about apples has made me hungry. Shall we go get one?

SNOW WHITE: As long as it's Poison Proof.

(*They exit, arm in arm. The* EVIL STEPMOTHER *and her attorney,* BERRY O. BLACKBIRD *enter.*)

EVIL STEPMOTHER: She did not really have the nerve to send me a coupon for Poison Proof Apples! You're my lawyer. Tell me what was that horrible stepdaughter of mine thinking?

BERRY BLACKBIRD: Maybe she thought you might like to eat an apple?

EVIL STEPMOTHER: That's ridiculous. And not only that, my staff tells me she hasn't taken the commercial off the air.

BERRY BLACKBIRD: Your staff told you? You don't watch TV?

EVIL STEPMOTHER: Of course not. There's nothing good on – except for my news show with what's her name – you know, she wears that hideous red cape? Never mind. But I also like Unlawful and Disorderly. They always track down the criminal and then show the trial and verdict.

BERRY BLACKBIRD: Maybe your case against her will be on it next season.

EVIL STEPMOTHER: Yes, (*taps her chin thoughtfully*) I'll call the producers in the morning.

BERRY BLACKBIRD: Who will you get to play me?

EVIL STEPMOTHER: Unless I don't sue her. I can always poison her again, or just cast a spell.

BERRY BLACKBIRD: But if you take her to court, you will be standing up for truth, justice and the fairy tale way.

EVIL STEPMOTHER: Who am I to argue with that? File the lawsuit!

BERRY BLACKBIRD: Okay.

EVIL STEPMOTHER: I want to teach that stepdaughter of mine a lesson once and for all. A lesson she won't forget. She'll learn that the law is even more potent than poison! (*cackles*)

EVIL STEPMOTHER and BERRY BLACKBIRD *exit.*

NARRATOR *enters stage right, or left, it doesn't matter as long as he or she gets on the stage.*

NARRATOR: Of course, the media had a field day with the story. But since The Evil Stepmother owned the only newspaper, the only television news program and the only radio station in Fairy Tale Land, the coverage wasn't exactly fair.

SNOW WHITE: (*calls from offstage*) Not as fair as my skin!

NARRATOR: Oh, thanks Snow White. I meant, the coverage wasn't exactly as fair as Snow White's skin.

NARRATOR *exits.* RED RIDING HOOD *and* WOLF *enter and sit on the chairs, papers in their hands, and* JACQUE *the cameraman stands off to the side a bit, holding a video camera.*

JACQUE: We'll be on in 60 seconds.

WOLF: How long is that exactly?

JACQUE: *(sighs)* One minute.

WOLF: That soon? Why'd you make it seem like we've got more time?

RED: I have the most lines so please keep the camera on me more than Big Bad.

WOLF: *(growls)* Stop calling me that. My professional name is Wolf.

RED: I don't know how you got this job anyway. Grandmother and I were doing fine as an anchor team until she disappeared.

WOLF: I had nothing to do with that. The x-ray cleared me, remember?

JACQUE: Thirty seconds. Stop the chit chat.

RED: I'm just giving this hound advice.

WOLF: I don't need advice. I've been in this business longer than you.

RED: I know. You're looking a bit grey.

WOLF: Why you little-

JACQUE: Five, four, two, three, one.

RED: *(smiles cheerily)* Good evening. Welcome to the Fairy Tale Land Evening News for Day 230, Year of the Magic Carpet. Our top story today – The Evil Stepmother has just sued Snow White for slander, libel and defamation of character.

WOLF: *(as he starts speaking, Jacque turns the camera his way)* It is alleged that Snow White cannot positively identify the alleged woman who gave her the allegedly poisoned apple.

RED: *(as she starts speaking Jacque turns the camera her way)* Doesn't look good for our fairy tale princess.

WOLF: *(as he starts speaking, Jacque turns the camera his way)* No, sure doesn't. Could Snow White be lying? Could she have been lying about everything all these years, including what she has for dinner?

RED: *(as she starts speaking Jacque turns the camera her way)* Just because you lie about that doesn't mean she does. Remember, the trial will be brought to you by me, Red Riding Hood, exclusively on this station because there isn't any other!

WOLF: (*as he starts speaking, Jacque turns the camera his way*) We'll be right back with a report on Jack Spriggins' arrest for trespassing, murder and possession of magic beans.

JACQUE: And we're clear.

RED: You camera hog! You took my lines!

WOLF: *Your* lines?

RED: At least you admit it. Don't let it happen again.

WOLF: *Again*?

RED: It's okay, you can stop apologizing now. I'm off to dinner with Jack Horner – he's taking me out for pie.

All three exit, BOY BLUE, *a radio talk show host comes on stage. He has a headset microphone and he sits on one of the chairs.* Callers *stand near the edge of the stage left or right, or even talk from the audience if the sound system allows.*

BOY BLUE: (*enthusiastically*) You're listening to the Boy Blue Talk Show on 9 and one eighth AM, where you do the talking and I'll be Blowing My Own Horn because, let's face it, no one can blow that horn like me. Our topic today is going to be, what else, the lawsuit against Snow White and I'm going to get right to the callers because my producer called me into his office this morning and told me that I talk too much. Can you believe it? The host of a talk show talks too much. What does he expect me to do, sing? Trust me, you don't want to hear me sing. Maybe if I would have had lessons as a child, but my parents were farmers and they kept telling me to watch the darn animals. Watch them do what, I always asked. I can't tell you how bore –what? (*he holds his ear piece*) Okay, okay, I'll get to the callers. The Muffin Man is on line one, calling from Drury Lane. You're on the air.

CALLER 1:   Yes, Blue, can you hear me? Hello?

BOY BLUE: I can hear you, you're on the air.

CALLER 1:   Yes, this is the Muffin Man on Drury Lane, and first I'd like to tell everyone that we're running a special on -.

BOY BLUE: (*interrupts*) Listen, man, don't turn this into a commercial. What do you want to share with the audience?

CALLER 1:   Well, first I'd like to say what an honor it is to speak with you.

BOY BLUE: I know. You are now among the privileged few who are allowed to speak on my show.

CALLER 1:   Second, I want to say how unfair this farce of a trial is.

BOY BLUE: (*he glances around before he answers a bit too loudly.*) You're right. Snow White should have stopped lying years ago.

CALLER 1:   I'm saying that the Evil Stepmother is making it a farce.

BOY BLUE: (*uncomfortably*) Yeah, Muffin Man, I hear you. We've all been talking about the Evil Stepmother. We're hoping she gets through this okay. Thanks for calling. Let's go to Line 1 for Peter Pumpkin Eater. Peter, you're on the air.

CALLER 2:   No, honey, stay in the pumpkin. You'll be fine. Oh, sorry, hello? Am I on the air?

BOY BLUE: You're on the air.

CALLER 2:   Hey, thanks Blue. Nice talking to you.

BOY BLUE: Sure is, isn't it? That's why I talk to myself so much. What's on your mind, Peter?

CALLER 2:   I called to let you know that I don't think Snow White is lying.

BOY BLUE: That's what I like. Sarcasm.

CALLER 2:   I'm not being sarcastic.

BOY BLUE: Ironic then. Just the right tone for this show. You're so funny.

CALLER 2:   How can people trust the Evil Stepmother. I mean, look at her name! What kind of person is called the Evil Stepmother?

BOY BLUE: Now you're just being silly. Stop using too many kinds of humor, it's annoying. Moving on to another caller. I didn't catch your name.

CALLER 3:   (*creepy voice*) You have three guesses. If you don't guess my name, I get your firstborn.

BOY BLUE: Hah! You can have him and good luck. Take his sister, too. Do you know what they've cost me in doctor's bills? Can't even fetch a pail of water without falling down. Next caller. Mary, you're on the air.

CALLER 4:   Blue, my lamb listens better than you do. We've been telling you that we believe Snow White.

BOY BLUE: We've sure had a bunch of jokers today.

CALLER 4:   I'm not joking. Are you on the Evil Stepmother's side just because she signs your paycheck?

BOY BLUE: That's got nothing to do with it. Time for a commercial – but not for Poison Proof Apples, I can tell you that. Stay tuned. We'll be right back and moving on to another topic. We'll be talking about that juvenile delinquent and a giant whose life wasn't worth beans.

BOY BLUE *exits stage left. The* EVIL STEPMOTHER *and* WILLIE ANN WINKIE *enter stage right. The* EVIL STEPMOTHER *sits on one of the chairs.*

WILLIE ANN WINKIE: (*scribbles away on her notepad*) Your Highness, what did you feel when you saw the commercial that calls you an attempted murderess?

THE EVIL STEPMOTHER: I could have cried. In fact, I'm sure I did.

WILLIE ANN WINKIE: Why would she say things like that about you?

EVIL STEPMOTHER: As a responsible -yet attractive- stepmother, I tried to set limits on her behavior. You might have heard that Snow White lured princes to the castle and then she ran off to live with seven horizontally challenged men. What's a stepmother to do?

WILLIE ANN WINKIE: What did you do?

EVIL STEPMOTHER: I sent a trusted employee to bring her heart – I mean, bring her back safe and sound, but she refused to cooperate.

WILLIE ANN WINKIE: Why have you filed a lawsuit against Snow White?

EVIL STEPMOTHER: My attorney, Berry Blackbird, said that I had to stand up for truth, justice and the fairy tale way, and who am I to argue with that?

WILLIE ANN WINKIE: What could Snow White do to make this up to you?

EVIL STEPMOTHER: I could just take her money and castle, but that's not enough. No, I want her to apologize to me in public, maybe on the show Unlawful and Disorderly, and on her knees and kissing the hem of my dress. Then, of course, I will forgive her because that's the kind of person I am.

WILLIE ANN WINKIE: What do you say about the witnesses who place you at the scene of Snow White's poisoning?

EVIL STEPMOTHER: Ms. Winkie, that's not one of the questions I gave you to ask. I think you have enough for the story – and let me proofread it before you turn it in. Never mind, I'll just write it myself. (*she grabs Willie's notepad*)

WILLIE ANN WINKIE: Don't the readers have the right to know the whole story?

EVIL STEPMOTHER: They have the right to know that I have been wrongfully accused of a crime. Not only that, the crime wasn't even successful, and I am successful in all that I do!

WILLIE ANN WINKIE: Wait, you're telling me that you're not guilty because you wouldn't have failed if you'd tried to poison Snow White?

EVIL STEPMOTHER: Yes, that's exactly what I'm saying, but with better sentence structure. Have schools today simply left out basic grammar? That's enough Ms. Winkie. You may go.

WILLIE ANN WINKIE: *shakes her head and exits, stage left.*

EVIL STEPMOTHER: The trial starts tomorrow and this time I won't rest until Snow White suffers as I have suffered all these years. She thinks she can get away with making a fool out of me! I'll show her.

That's the **end** *of* **ACT I.**

ACT II.

The scene is a Courtroom. JUDGE THUMBELINA *sits in the Judge spot, with a witness chair beside her.* MS. BLACKBIRD, THE EVIL STEPMOTHER, MR. FOX, *Snow White's attorney, and* SNOW WHITE *sit at their respective tables in front of JUDGE THUMBELINA. Witnesses come on stage when called.*

JUDGE THUMBELINA: Good Morning. Is my microphone on? Can you hear me? This is Case No. 987654321, The Evil Stepmother v. Snow White and Poison Proof Apples, Inc. Go ahead, Ms. Blackbird, I believe you get to go first.

MS. BLACKBIRD: Thank you. Our case is actually quite simple. Snow White made a commercial that clearly says that The Evil Stepmother tried to kill her with a poisoned apple.

SNOW WHITE: That's right. She did.

JUDGE THUMBELINA: Please, it's not your turn to talk, dear.

SNOW WHITE: Your Highness.

JUDGE THUMBELINA: No, your Honor.

SNOW WHITE: I beg your pardon?

JUDGE THUMBELINA: That's all right. Just don't interrupt again. Please continue, Ms. Blackbird.

MS. BLACKBIRD: She said that lie to hurt her stepmother and ruin her reputation, her business and her life. However, if Snow White really thought her stepmother tried to kill her, she would have pressed charges, but she never did. Snow White knows that there is no proof that her stepmother did these things, indeed is incapable of acting in such a manner, being such a kind, gentle and loving woman.

SNOW WHITE: She's a what?

JUDGE THUMBELINA: (*smacks her gavel*) Order! Don't make me smack this gavel against you again.

SNOW WHITE: (*puts her hand over her mouth and shakes her head*)

MS. BLACKBIRD: Snow White is guilty and should be punished by throwing her in jail, taking away her Fairy Tale Princess title, and making her apologize on television during the final taping of Unlawful and Disorderly. Snow White lied about her stepmother poisoning her with an apple and that The Evil Stepmother is a pitiable victim in this tragic case.

JUDGE THUMBELINA: Thank you, Ms. Blackbird. If this is true, no wonder the Evil Stepmother had to sue. Your turn, Mr. Fox. Hope you've got a good explanation for your client's actions. I mean, Snow White looks like a very nice fairy tale princess, but if she really lied, well –tsk, tsk.

MR. FOX: Your Honor, all we have to say is that Snow White did not lie, and we can prove it.

MS. BLACKBIRD: Yeah, right.

JUDGE THUMBELINA: Ms. Blackbird, call your first witness.

MS. BLACKBIRD: My first witness is Mrs. Susan Lace.

SUE LACE: (*comes to the stand*)

MS. BLACKBIRD: Mrs. Lace, please state your name for the record.

SUE LACE: Susan Lace. But please, just call me Sue.

MS. BLACKBIRD: Mrs. Lace, where do you reside?

SUE LACE: I live in a shoe. But really, you can call me Sue. It's okay.

MS. BLACKBIRD: Mrs. Lace, are you married?

SUE LACE: Yes, but my husband is away at sea a lot. I think he leaves me alone with all our children on purpose.

MS. BLACKBIRD: Do you have children?

SUE LACE: I just said – yes, I have so many children I don't know what to do.

MS. BLACKBIRD: What is your occupation?

SUE LACE: I'm a mother. That's a lot of occupation. Have you tried to keep up with laundry for a dozen people? No, wait, I think I just had another one recently. Yes, I did, but now that I think about it, it was twins. Or does it just seem like it?

MS. BLACKBIRD: Were you ever employed by the Evil Stepmother?

SUE LACE: Oh! I see what you're getting at. Yes, I was Snow White's nanny.

MS. BLACKBIRD: Was Snow White a good girl when she was small?

SUE LACE: Sure she was. But she was an only child. Who's she going to fight with?

MS. BLACKBIRD: Was she rebellious when she was a teenager?

SUE LACE: Not really –(*glances at the Evil Stepmother*) I mean, yes.

MS. BLACKBIRD: Did the Evil Stepmother do her best to make Snow White behave?

SUE LACE: I really didn't see (*glances at Evil Stepmother again*)– I mean, yes, of course.

MS. BLACKBIRD: Did Snow White run away?

SUE LACE: Yes. Uh huh. That she did. Ran away.

MS. BLACKBIRD: And you know that the Evil Stepmother decided to go away for about a year because of the stress around the time that Snow White fell into the alleged coma?

SUE LACE: Yes.

MR. FOX: Objection. Leading the witness.

MS. BLACKBIRD: I'm just asking questions, Your Honor.

JUDGE THUMBELINA: Overruled, keep going Ms. Blackbird.

MS. BLACKBIRD: Thank you. Did she go away to the Sunny Valley Spa to relieve her stress?

SUE LACE: Yes.

MS. BLACKBIRD: Did the Evil Stepmother ever try to kill Snow White with a poisoned apple?

SUE LACE: No.

MS. BLACKBIRD: I pass this witness.

JUDGE THUMBELINA: Your witness, Mr. Fox.

MR. FOX: Mrs. Lace – Sue, you said that Snow White was rebellious as a teenager. In what way?

SUE LACE: What do you mean?

MR. FOX: Did she talk back to her stepmother?

SUE LACE: Yes.

MR. FOX: Did she get bad grades?

SUE LACE: Yes.

MR. FOX: Did she keep her room clean?

SUE LACE: Yes.

MR. FOX: Did The Evil Stepmother threaten you?

SUE LACE: Yes. Oh, I mean –

THE EVIL STEPMOTHER: (*starts to rise from her chair, then sits back down*)

SUE LACE: No, no, she would –no. (*starts crying*)

MS. BLACKBIRD: Objection!

JUDGE THUMBELINA: Are you able to continue, Mrs. Lace?

SUE LACE: (*shakes head*)

MR. FOX: I'm finished with this witness, your Honor.

JUDGE THUMBELINA: You may step down, Mrs. Lace.

SUE LACE *steps down, and goes stage right, and meets* WILLIE ANN WINKIE

WILLIE ANN WINKIE: (*speaks while writing on note pad*) This reporter has just discovered that Mrs. Lace, retired royal nanny, had been charged with being unreasonably mean to her children for spanking them when they misbehaved and feeding them bread without any broth.

SUE LACE: (*wiping her eyes with a hanky*) They're lucky they got that, the little hooligans!

WILLIE ANN WINKIE: What do you say to those who think spanking is a bad idea?

SUE LACE: (*more firmly, tears are gone*) You try having all those children underfoot! They're always fighting and they never pick up after themselves.

WILLIE ANN WINKIE: Have you tried rewarding them for good behavior? You know, giving them gold stickers for good behavior?

SUE LACE: Hah! Negative reinforcement is the only way to go.

They both exit stage left, still chatting about punishment.

JUDGE THUMBELINA: Ms. Blackbird, please call your next witness.

MS. BLACKBIRD: The Plaintiff calls Jack Horner to the stand.

JACK HORNER *(comes to the stand)*

MS.BLACKBIRD: Please state your name for the record.

JACK HORNER: Jack Horner.

MS. BLACKBIRD: Are you married?

JACK HORNER: No. I'd started thinking about marriage because I had a girlfriend until breakfast – a real pretty one, too, but she just broke up with me. I don't know what happened. I thought Red Riding Hood enjoyed pies as much as I do. *(holds his hand over his heart and look sad)* I'm sorry, it's a difficult time for me.

MS. BLACKBIRD: What is your occupation?

JACK HORNER: I started my own business - Jack Horner's Toxin Corner- and I mainly analyze fruit. My specialty is plums, but I do all kinds.

MS. BLACKBIRD: Did the Evil Stepmother and I recently employ you?

JACK HORNER: Yes. I analyzed a bit of old apple.

MS. BLACKBIRD: What did you look for in that piece of apple?

JACK HORNER: Poison. I checked for things like arsenic, paint thinner, and the worst of them all - broccoli. Came up clean though.

MS. BLACKBIRD: So, the apple was non-poisonous.

JACK HORNER: Still wouldn't make a good pie filling. Too hard.

MS. BLACKBIRD: Thank you, Mr. Horner. Your witness, Mr. Fox.

MR. FOX: Mr. Horner, did you check for eye of newt?

JACK HORNER: No.

MR. FOX: How about toe of frog?

JACK HORNER: No.

MR. FOX: Or spleen of pufferfish?

JACK HORNER: No.

MR. FOX: Why not?

JACK HORNER: Those aren't traditional poisons.

MR. FOX: Oh?

JACK HORNER: Of course, come to think about it, if they were combined they could put a person right out.

MR. FOX: What about if you put them together with a spell?

JACK HORNER: Whoa. Yes, then for sure.

MR. FOX: Thank you, Mr. Horner.

MS. BLACKBIRD: (*Stands*) Redirect. Mr. Horner, did you find any spell residue in that apple?

JACK HORNER: No, but there's no way to check for that as far as I know.

MS. BLACKBIRD: That is all. Thank you, Mr. Horner.

LITTLE JACK HORNER *steps down and goes stage right, and meets* WILLIE ANN WINKIE.

WILLIE ANN WINKIE: Mr. Horner, I'd like to interview you for the Fairy Tale Tattler. I'm writing a series of articles about Snow White's trial.

JACK HORNER: I'm sorry, I'm not going to be a good interview right now. Broken heart you know.

WILLIE ANN WINKIE: Oh, so you're unattached?

JACK HORNER: I'd really like to help you with your articles. It's not you, you're a lovely reporter. I mean, lovely in the sense that you're very pretty, not in your writing. Not that your writing isn't lovely, it's very readable, but writing isn't called lovely as a rule. Unless it's poetry –

WILLIE ANN WINKIE: I'm not usually so forward, but how about meeting me later at BoPeep's Bistro? No interview, just a pie and some company?

JACK HORNER: That would be nice. How about now? Let's go now. (*they walk off stage together*) You like pie? What's your favorite?

MS. BLACKBIRD: The Plaintiff calls Dr. Foster to the stand.

DR FOSTER: (*comes to the stand*)

MS. BLACKBIRD: You are the doctor that treated The Evil Stepmother twenty years ago for her injuries at Sunny Valley Nursing Facility, is that correct?

DR. FOSTER: Yes. It's actually the Sunny Valley Spa and Clinic.

MS. BLACKBIRD: Can you tell me what she looked like when she arrived at your clinic?

DR. FOSTER: Yes, I can. She looked about the same as she does now.

MS. BLACKBIRD: So she didn't look like an old crone?

DR. FOSTER: Ha ha. No. And with proper diet, exercise and plastic spellery she will always look good. That's one of the things we teach at the clinic.

MS. BLACKBIRD: What was she treated for at your clinic?

DR. FOSTER: She was treated for stress. However, she did have minor injuries that were sustained during an accident on the way to the clinic.

MR. FOX: What were these injuries?

DR. FOSTER: I don't remember.

MS. BLACKBIRD: How long was she at the clinic?

DR. FOSTER: Again, I don't remember. It was so long ago. But we usually keep patients for at least six months for the full treatment.

MS. BLACKBIRD: But you are sure that The Evil Stepmother was admitted, and not an old peddler woman.

DR. FOSTER: Ha ha. No. Generally peddler women cannot afford our prices.

(*General Laughter in the Court Room*)

JUDGE THUMBELINA: Order! That's enough. It wasn't that funny.

MS. BLACKBIRD: Sorry, your Honor. I'm finished with this witness.

JUDGE THUMBELINA: Mr. Fox, your turn.

MR. FOX: Thank you, your Honor. Now, Dr. Foster, how long have you worked at this clinic?

DR. FOSTER: About twenty-five years.

MR. FOX: How many patients would you say you've had?

DR. FOSTER: A great deal.

MR. FOX: Did you treat the giant that fell off the beanstalk?

DR. FOSTER: I performed the autopsy.

MR. FOX: How is he doing now?

DR. FOSTER: He's dead.

MR. FOX: Indeed? And what about Cinderella's family?

DR. FOSTER: I was their family physician.

MR. FOX: And how is Cinderella's mother now?

DR FILBEDDER: She's dead.

MR. FOX: What did you tell Aunt Rhody?

DR. FOSTER: Her old grey goose was dead.

MR. FOX: Really? And how about Humpty Dumpty? Could you put him together again?

DR. FOSTER: No. But that's not --

MR. FOX: Of course it isn't. Where is your clinic located?

DR. FOSTER: In Diamond Hills.

MR. FOX: Isn't that pretty close to the dwarves' cottage?

DR. FOSTER: I wouldn't know.

MR. FOX: You said the Evil Stepmother arrived injured. Would she have been able to get to your clinic without assistance?

DR. FOSTER: I- -I don't--that is, I'm sure that --maybe.

MR. FOX: I mean, wherever her accident happened, I'm sure she could have even crawled to your clinic for help.

DR. FOSTER: I don't understand --.

MR. FOX: Did the Evil Stepmother have a reservation at your clinic or did she just show up unannounced?

MS. BLACKBIRD: Objection.

JUDGE THUMBELINA: Whatever for? You may answer, Dr. Foster.

DR. FOSTER: I don't know if she had a reservation. I don't handle admissions. I am a doctor.

MR. FOX: I'm quite through with this witness.

MS. BLACKBIRD: Redirect, your Honor?

JUDGE THUMBELINA: Of course. You want to head him north again? Haha.

MS. BLACKBIRD: What?

JUDGE THUMBELINA: Redirect? Head him north? (*no one laughs*) Never mind. Continue.

MS. BLACKBIRD: Dr. Foster. Once again, for the record, did you ever see the Evil Stepmother looking like an old peddler woman?

DR. FOSTER: Never.

MS. BLACKBIRD: That is all.

JUDGE THUMBELINA: Thank you, Dr. Foster. You may step down.

DR. FOSTER: If I might add something, Your Honor.

JUDGE THUMBELINA: Of course, doctor.

DR. FOSTER: Can you have someone fill in those huge holes in the street outside the courtroom. If it rains, they're going to make dangerous puddles. Someone could get hurt.

JUDGE THUMBELINA: I'm sorry?

DR. FOSTER: You see, I once went to Gloster and I stepped in a deep puddle and I'm never going there again.

JUDGE THUMBELINA: I'll take it under advisement.

DR. FOSTER: Thank you. (*steps down, exits*)

JUDGE THUMBELINA: Ms. Blackbird, call your next witness.

MS. BLACKBIRD: We only have one more, Your Honor. The prosecution would like to call Snow White.

General surprised murmuring in courtroom.

MR. FOX: (*shouts*) Objection! Objection!

JUDGE THUMBELINA: Sorry, Mr. Fox. I'll allow it.

SNOW WHITE: (*goes to witness stand*)

MS. BLACKBIRD: Please state your name for the record.

SNOW WHITE: (*looks around in surprise*) We're being recorded? Where's the camera?

MS. BLACKBIRD: There is no camera.

SNOW WHITE: Just a tape recorder.

MS. BLACKBIRD: What I mean is – yes, that's it. You are Snow White, is that correct?

SNOW WHITE: Is that a trick question?

MS. BLACKBIRD: Please tell me about your stepmother. How did she treat you when you were a teenager?

SNOW WHITE: She kept me pretty busy with chores around the castle.

MS. BLACKBIRD: Was your life ever in danger?

SNOW WHITE: I suppose I could have swallowed the cleanser if I wasn't paying attention.

MS. BLACKBIRD: I meant, did she ever threaten your life?

SNOW WHITE: Not until she told the huntsman to kill me.

MS. BLACKBIRD: If she did tell him to do that, he didn't kill you, is that correct?

SNOW WHITE: You can't tell? I know my skin is as white as snow, but I don't think I look like a corpse.

MS. BLACKBIRD: No, you look as beautiful as ever. My question was –

SNOW WHITE: Thank you.

MS. BLACKBIRD: -why didn't he kill you if that was what he was sent to do?

SNOW WHITE: He said he couldn't and I didn't want to argue with him about it.

MS. BLACKBIRD: Then you lived with several small men? *Alone*?

SNOW WHITE: Seven dwarves. I kept house for them while they mined diamonds.

MS. BLACKBIRD: You stayed with them how long?

SNOW WHITE: Until my stepmother disguised herself as an old woman and gave me a poisoned apple.

MS. BLACKBIRD: Did you know it was your stepmother disguised as an old woman?

SNOW WHITE: Not then.

MS. BLACKBIRD: When did you know?

SNOW WHITE: As soon as I was poisoned by the apple.

MS. BLACKBIRD   Did the old woman say she was your stepmother?

SNOW WHITE: No.

MS. BLACKBIRD: Did she look like your stepmother?

SNOW WHITE: Of course not. That's why it's called a disguise.

MS. BLACKBIRD: Then how would you know it was your stepmother?

SNOW WHITE: Who else could it have been?

MS. BLACKBIRD: Could it have been only an old woman?

SNOW WHITE: Yes. My stepmother disguised as an old woman.

MS. BLACKBIRD: But you just said that she didn't look like your stepmother and didn't say she was your stepmother so how can you be sure that it was your stepmother?

SNOW WHITE: No one else had ever tried to kill me.

MS. BLACKBIRD: How do you know that?

SNOW WHITE: How do I know what?

MS. BLACKBIRD: That no one else had ever tried to kill you?

SNOW WHITE: That's a silly question.

MS. BLACKBIRD: Can you answer it?

SNOW WHITE: I thought I did.

MS. BLACKBIRD: No, you did not.

SNOW WHITE: I am sorry.

MS. BLACKBIRD: Please answer the question.

SNOW WHITE: Okay.

MS. BLACKBIRD: Okay what?

SNOW WHITE: I'll answer the question.

MS. BLACKBIRD   Go ahead. Answer it.

SNOW WHITE: I thought I did. What was it again?

MS. BLACKBIRD   Let's just move on. Why didn't you press charges against your stepmother for attempted murder?

SNOW WHITE: The dwarves saw her go over a cliff and they thought she was dead. By the time we realized she was alive, I was already living happily ever after, and a murder trial would have ruined that.

MS. BLACKBIRD: Let's go to the commercial. In that commercial you state that you were poisoned by your stepmother. Isn't that correct?

SNOW WHITE: Yes.

MS. BLACKBIRD: But you can't prove that it was your stepmother, isn't that correct?

SNOW WHITE: I don't have to prove it. Everyone knows it.

MS. BLACKBIRD   Your Highness, have you ever considered the possibility that it wasn't your stepmother who gave you that poisoned apple?

SNOW WHITE: No, because it was my stepmother.

MS. BLACKBIRD: What if you've been maligning her wrongfully all these years?

SNOW WHITE: If you're saying that I've been talking bad about her and she hasn't done anything, then no, because she did.

MS. BLACKBIRD: I sent you a letter asking you to stop making the commercial because it was hurting your stepmother's feelings and business but the commercial continued to air and therefore continued to libel and slander the Evil Stepmother.

SNOW WHITE: How can it be libel and slander if it's true?

MS. BLACKBIRD   Libel and slander are serious allegations, your Highness. You may have ruined your stepmother's life over something of which she is innocent.

SNOW WHITE: But she's not.

MS. BLACKBIRD: Your Highness, thank you for your time. The Prosecution rests, your Honor.

JUDGE THUMBELINA: Oh, good, just in time for dinner. So tomorrow we have the Defense witnesses. Who do you have scheduled, Mr. Fox?

MR. FOX: The seven dwarves are first.

JUDGE THUMBELINA: Are you going to have them testify as a group or one at a time?

MR. FOX: One at a time.

JUDGE THUMBELINA: Anyone else?

MR. FOX: The huntsman.

EVIL STEPMOTHER: That traitor!

MS. BLACKBIRD: (*shakes her head and puts her hand on the* EVIL STEPMOTHER'S *arm, but pulls it off quickly as if she had been burned.*)

JUDGE THUMBELINA: Sounds like a full day. We'd better adjourn court for the night.

SNOW WHITE: (*starts to get up*)

JUDGE THUMBELINA: Wait! No-one gets to leave until I smack my gavel. That's my favorite part of the job. (*smacks gavel*). Okay, court is recessed. Now you can go.
(*Curtain closes or everyone exits and then RED RIDING HOOD comes on stage, with a microphone. The CAMERAMAN is filing her and a line of women come onstage*)

RED RIDING HOOD: Good Morning, Fairy Tale Land. This is Red Riding Hood, reporting live for Channel 1 from the dwarves cottage. Several hours ago, it was learned that the huntsman has disappeared and the dwarves were discovered unconscious in their dining room. It is rumored that the dwarves ate poisoned applesauce, given to them by a peddler woman. Unfortunately, the trial continues in less than an hour and it is doubtful that the huntsman will be found and the dwarves will probably not be awake to testify in Snow White's defense by then.

TROLL WOMAN: At least one of them will be there if I have anything to say about it!

RED RIDING HOOD: As we all know, the dwarves can only be awoke by love's true kiss—

TROLL WOMAN: Don't you mean awaked?

DWARF WOMAN: I think the correct word is awakened.

RED RIDING HOOD: (*ignores everyone*) …can only be revived by love's true kiss.
TROLL WOMAN: I'm pretty sure that it's true love's kiss. Love doesn't have a true kiss, per se. Does that mean some kisses can be false?

DWARF WOMAN: What the heck are you talking about?

RED RIDING HOOD: (*still ignoring them*) …although the dwarves have never been known as romantic heroes, as you can see, that hasn't stopped hundreds of ladies who are lined up to give those sleeping dwarves a hopeful peck on the cheek.. I think Snow White needs more than a good attorney right now. She needs a fairy godmother. Back to Wolf at the studio.

Lights out over RED RIDING HOOD, TROLL WOMAN and DWARF WOMAN. *Lights on stage right over Snow White.*

SNOW WHITE: Good idea. I'm calling for a fairy godmother. (*stands there, listening, then pressing a button on her cell phone, then listens. She repeats this activity 5 times, then leaves a message*.) This is Snow White and I'm really worried about the trial. If someone could come right away I'd appreciate it because I'm going to court but none of my witnesses can testify and I'm not sure if even Mr. Fox is going to be able to pull this off now. I'm in Judge Thumbelina's courtroom so please come and help. Thank you."

SNOW WHITE *exits, light goes out*

This is the **End** *of* **Act II**

Act III

Curtain opens on everyone in their places in the courtroom again.

JUDGE THUMBELINA: We're back on the record. I understand that you don't have any witnesses anymore, Mr. Fox. What are you planning to do?

MR. FOX: I'd like to call a hostile witness. The Evil Stepmother.

MS. BLACKBIRD: Objection!

JUDGE THUMBELINA: Object? Why?

MS. BLACKBIRD: The Evil Stepmother is not hostile. She's a very agreeable woman.

JUDGE THUMBELINA: That's the most ridiculous thing I've heard since breakfast. Objection overruled.

EVIL STEPMOTHER: (*goes to witness stand*)

MR. FOX: Evil Stepmother, I understand that you did not expect to be a witness today. It's just that I need someone to clarify matters.

EVIL STEPMOTHER: I'm glad to cooperate in any way I can.

MR. FOX: Have you ever tried to harm Snow White?

EVIL STEPMOTHER: Of course not. There's nothing like family.

MR. FOX: How did you get along?

EVIL STEPMOTHER: Very well until she became a teenager, and she became very interested in boys. I remember one incident in which she lured a wandering prince from the forest to her balcony.

MR. FOX: What did you do when she acted like this?

EVIL STEPMOTHER: I tried to keep her too busy for mischief, by making her do menial tasks, but she ran off anyway. I was heartbroken, but fortunately I am even more beautiful when I am sad.

MR. FOX: Do you have a magic mirror, your Highness?

EVIL STEPMOTHER: I did have one, but I bro-- it cracked and does not show reflections accurately anymore.

MR. FOX: Did this magic mirror state one day that Snow White was more beautiful than you?

EVIL STEPMOTHER: Actually, the mirror said that she was the *fairest*, which is completely different from beautiful. No one is more beautiful than me. Snow White is just very pale.

MR. FOX: Did you ever disguise yourself as an old hag?

EVIL STEPMOTHER: That is ridiculous. It is not possible to make myself look ugly.

MR. FOX: So, you're saying that you didn't.

EVIL STEPMOTHER: That is what I am saying, but with better enunciation and grammar.

MR. FOX: Did you ever go to the dwarves' residence?

EVIL STEPMOTHER: You mean those seven vertically challenged individuals in that cramped little cottage across that rickety bridge deep in the Enchanted Forest? Of course not.

MR. FOX: Did you ever give Snow White a poisoned apple?

EVIL STEPMOTHER: No.

MR. FOX: Did you ever spend any time in the hospital?

EVIL STEPMOTHER: No. I'm never sick.

MR. FOX: Then how do you account for your stay at the Sunny Valley Spa and Nursing Facility?

EVIL STEPMOTHER: What?

MR. FOX: Remember yesterday when Dr. Foster testified that you were at Sunny Valley and according to the records, you were diagnosed with three broken ribs, a broken arm and a ruptured spleen.

EVIL STEPMOTHER: Oh, that. I said I was never sick, not that I was never injured on the way to the Spa for treatment of stress.

MR. FOX: What happened when Snow White made those commercials that said you poisoned her?

THE EVIL STEPMOTHER: I cried huge, diamond like tears.

MR. FOX: Then what did you do?

EVIL STEPMOTHER: My attorney requested Snow White to stop the commercial.

MR. FOX: Did you ever try to kill her?

EVIL STEPMOTHER: Me personally, of course not.

MR. FOX: Not you personally? So that means you sent someone else out to kill her?

EVIL STEPMOTHER: Stop twisting my words.

MR. FOX: You became a stepmother to a young girl who was becoming more beautiful each day. You couldn't let that happen. So you first sent the huntsman out to kill Snow White, but he couldn't do it, so you poisoned an apple and disguised yourself and gave that apple to your stepdaughter.

EVIL STEPMOTHER: So you say, but you don't have me on tape doing any of those things. You have no witnesses, no evidence. (*turns to* JUDGE THUMBELINA) I'm afraid they're out of luck. Can you declare me the winner and we can go home?

WOMAN IN LONG FLOWING ROBES WHO JUST BURST IN THE COURTROOM DOOR: Someone called for a fairy godmother?

MAN IN BACK ROW ON RIGHT: I did.

WOMAN IN SECOND TO FRONT ROW ON LEFT: No, it was me.

CHILD STANDING IN BACK: Me!

YOUNG LADY: I called for one last week.

WOMAN IN LONG FLOWING ROBES: Are any of you Snow White?

SNOW WHITE: That's me. I'm up here.

WOMAN IN LONG FLOWING ROBES: Hi, I'm Bernice, I'll be your fairy godmother for today. You asked for help with the trial?

SNOW WHITE: That's right.

MS. BLACKBIRD: Objection! This woman has no business being in this courtroom during a trial.

JUDGE THUMBELINA: She *is* a Fairy Godmother and we *are* in Fairy Tale Land. I'll allow it.

BERNICE: Thank you, your Honor. Mr. Fox, here is evidence that will clear your client. (*hands* JUDGE THUMBELINA *a VCR tape*)

MR. FOX: A tape?

FAIRY GODMOTHER: We have it on DVD, too, if you prefer. We even have different versions of the same event, different production companies, but in each one you'll see The Evil Stepmother trying to kill Snow White.

EVIL STEPMOTHER: I knew I should have poisoned that horrible cameraman with that apple I gave to Snow White –uh, oh. (Claps her hand over her mouth.)

MS. BLACKBIRD: Objection! Let her last statement be stricken from the record.

JUDGE THUMBELINA: Overruled.

MR. FOX: Motion to declare The Evil Stepmother guilty of attempted murder.

JUDGE THUMBELINA: Granted.

MS. BLACKBIRD: Objection.

JUDGE THUMBELINA: Overruled.

THE EVIL STEPMOTHER: Noooooooooooooooooo!

MR. FOX: Motion for everyone to live happily ever after.

JUDGE THUMBELINA: Everyone except the Evil Stepmother! Bailiff, take her away. Snow White, you are free to go. Court is adjourned.

SNOW WHITE: Thank you, your honor. Thank you, Fairy Godmother.

BERNICE: I'll send you my bill.

General Celebration in courtroom! YAY!

As the curtain starts to close, NARRATOR *comes on stage right.*

NARRATOR: And of course they all lived happily ever after, whatever that really means. Thank you all for coming tonight and if you'll all depart alphabetically, that would be great. Those of you whose last names start with the letter A go first-

SNOW WHITE: *(runs on stage)* Wait! We're not quite done.

NARRATOR: What are you talking about? The curtain closed, and I get the audience out so everyone can get everyone can start living happily ever after.

SNOW WHITE: You can't make them leave just yet. I think we're supposed to bow and curtsy and they're supposed to applaud.

NARRATOR: That's not in the script. Do they know when to applaud?

SNOW WHITE: Yes, they do. They're a very smart audience.

NARRATOR: What if they don't?

SNOW WHITE: Then fairies won't get their wings.

NARRATOR: That's a new one. Okay, everyone, time for the clapping, bowing and curtsying.

SNOW WHITE: *(starts running off stage, then stops and turns to the audience.)* Wait, don't clap too hard, I don't want anyone's palms to get sore. *(Runs off stage.)*

Curtain reopens. All characters on stage, bowing and curtsying and the audience will applaud. Really they will. It's a habit.

THE END

Curtains close, audience and cast exits to go live happily ever after.

Supplemental Documents

THE FAIRYTALE TATTLER

www.tattler.tale   Day 149, Year of the Magic Carpet   150

THE CUPBOARD IS BARE!

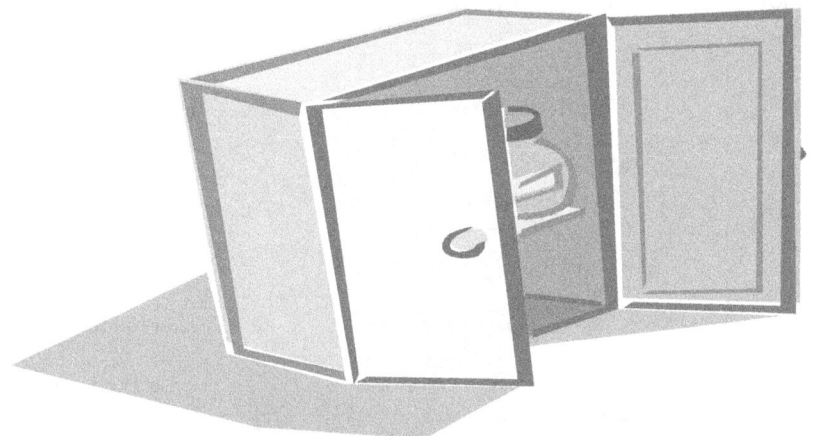

Says O.M. Hubbard, Chairperson of the Fairy Tale Land Reserve

KING LEE WILL SAVE LAND FROM BANKRUPTCY!

SHEEP MISSING!
BOPEEP PLEADS ACCOUNTING ERROR

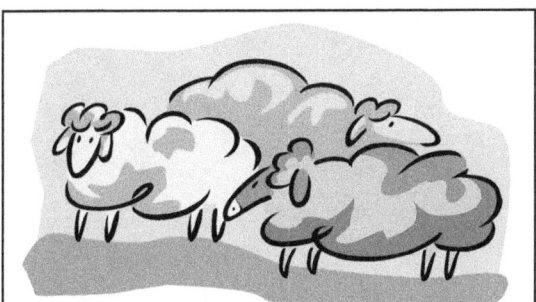

NEW STUDY: PRINCESSES FREQUENTLY IN DANGER;
Prince Will vows to rescue at least one.

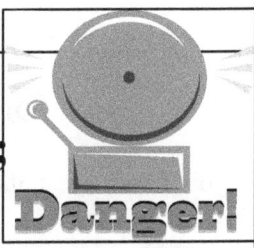

HUMPTY FALLS:
Egg Drop SOUP Added To Soldiers' Rations

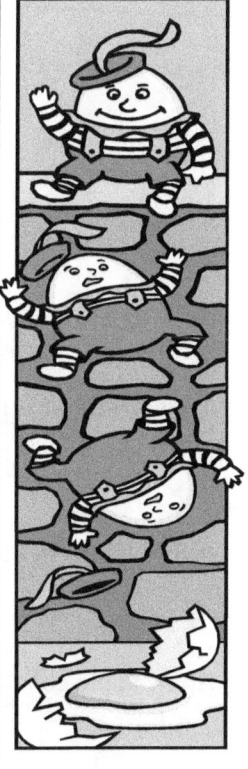

Commercial Taping: Poison Proof Apples, Inc.
Day 175, Year of the Magic Carpet

Shot number	Screen Image	Audio/text
1	Best Red Apple close-up With Poison Proof Sticker	Jingle Tune ('Apple, apple' Sung by Snow White)
2	External Shot of Apple Orchard	"Apple apple…" Snow White begins to sing
3	Close up of Snow White	"…good for you…"
4	Snow White slowly brings the apple to her face as she sings	"…lasts a year…"
5	Snow White prepares to eat apple	"…tastes like new."
6	Snow White takes a big bite of apple.	Jingle tune in full orchestra
7	Snow White shows apple with bite taken out, says,	"Don't make the same mistake I did and eat an ordinary apple poisoned by *your* evil stepmother. Buy Poison Proof Apple Brand, the only apples grown in the Enchanted Orchard."
8	Close up of Snow White smiling, says,	"Potion repellant and oh, so tasty, too."
9	Fade in of apple only	Text (in caps): 'POISON PROOF APPLES'

The Optional Jingles for the Commercial

Jingles:

"Apple apple from the tree. Tastes so good and good for me."

Or

"Apple apple such good fruit. Full of fiber, makes you toot."

Or

"Apple apple good for you. Lasts a year and tastes like new."

909 Black Ridge Road   **BLACKBIRD & CROW, P.C.**
Fairy Tale Land   *Smart Lawyers who look good in black*
Telephone: 99999
Fax: 99991

Internet: blackbird&crow@darkcolors.com

Berry O. Blackbird

Day 190, Year of the Magic Carpet

Snow White, Fairy Tale Princess   **BY PIGEON POST**
The Castle on the Hill
Fairy Tale Land

Re: Commercial for Poison Proof Brand Apples

Dear Your Highness:

I am Queen Endora's lawyer. This letter is to inform you that she has asked me to tell you that your commercial is hurting her feelings and it is also against the law. She cannot believe that you really think she tried to poison you with an apple. If you do not stop airing this commercial, I am authorized to file suit against you for defamation of character, slander and libel.

Very truly yours,

Berry O. Blackbird

BOB/jay

cc: Queen Endora

The Castle On The Hill

A Message from Snow White

Day 195, Year of the Magic Carpet

Berry Blackbird, Esq.
Blackbird & Crow, P.C.
909 Black Ridge Road
Fairy Tale Land

Dear Ms. Blackbird:

Thank you for your letter to Snow White. Unfortunately, the enormous amount of fan mail that our favorite fairy tale princess receives makes it impossible for her to reply to everyone individually and she would like to remind you that she does not accept unsolicited gifts of any sort. However, she wishes you the best. Thank you again for taking the time to write her a letter.

Sincerely,

Gretel W. Piperson

Assistant to Snow White

IN THE FAIRY TALE DISTRICT COURT
ONCE UPON A TIME DIVISION

QUEEN ENDORA a/k/a The Evil Stepmother,	:	
	:	
	:	**CASE NO. 987654321**
Plaintiff,	:	
	:	
vs.	:	
	:	
SNOW WHITE and	:	
POISON PROOF APPLES, INC.,	:	
	:	
Defendants	:	
_____	:	

PLAINTIFF'S ORIGINAL PETITION

TO THE HONORABLE COURT:

NOW COMES Queen Endora a/k/a "The Evil Stepmother", as Plaintiff, and files

Plaintiff's Original Petition in which it complains of Snow White and Poison Proof Apples,

Inc., Defendants. Queen Endora would show the Court as follows:

Jurisdiction
I.

This Court has jurisdiction under the provisions of Liar Liar Pants on Fire Code of

Bad Conduct No. 12, Article 3, § 54.

Parties

Plaintiff

II.

Plaintiff is Queen Endora, "The Evil Stepmother."

Defendant

III

Defendant Snow White is a Fairy Tale Princess and stepdaughter to Plaintiff Queen

Endora.

IV.

Defendant Poison Proof Apples, Inc. is a corporation that sells apples in Fairy Tale Land.

General Facts Underlying Suit

V.

Long ago, Queen Endora became a stepmother to Snow White.

VI.

Although sweet natured and obedient in her childhood, Snow White became rebellious and uncontrollable during her teenage years and ran off with a huntsman and eventually ended up living with several horizontally challenged men.

VII.

Snow White, on or about Day 79, Year of the Fairy Godmother, ate an apple, choked and lost consciousness, but was rescued by the handsome Prince who dislodged the section of apple that was stuck in her throat.

VIII.

On or about Day 100, year of the Magic Carpet, Snow White began appearing in commercials sponsored by Poison Proof Apples, Inc., in which Snow White states that the apple she choked on had been poisoned by her stepmother, and this statement falsely charges Plaintiff with a crime.

IX.

Snow White made those statements with malice, knowing them to be lies.

Actual Damages

X

After the commercials aired, Queen Endora has been exposed to public hatred, contempt, and ridicule, resulting in really hurt feelings and a damaged reputation in the business world.

XI

As a result, Queen Endora lost not only social standing, but also self-esteem and an estimated monetary sum of way more than you can count.

WHEREFORE PREMISES CONSIDERED, Plaintiff requests trial and that Snow White be cited to appear, answer and upon final hearing Plaintiff have judgment.

Respectfully submitted,

_____
Berry O. Blackbird

BLACKBIRD AND CROW, P.C.
Attorneys at Law
909 Black Ridge Road   ATTORNEY FOR PLAINTIFF
Fairy Tale Land   QUEEN ENDORA
                                                        "THE EVIL STEPMOTHER"
Telephone: 99999
FAX: 99991

"I AM NOT A WITCH!"
by
Willie Ann Winkie, Reporter for the Fairy Tale Tattler

"No, really," insisted Queen Endora, a/k/a "The Evil Stepmother," at an exclusive interview with this reporter at the valiant Queen's residence, the Magnificent Castle. Looking as lovely as usual, the courageous Queen revealed her feelings upon seeing the commercial that labeled her an attempted murderess of her beloved stepdaughter, Snow White.

"I could have cried. In fact, I'm sure I did," the charming Queen said in a tremulous voice as this reporter saw her bravely hold back a single tear drop in the corner of her left eye. "I cannot believe that my stepdaughter would say those lies about me for everyone to hear. I have never tried to poison Snow White, let alone kill her! I am devastated."

Queen Endora had no idea why Snow White would hate her so much as to lie about her, but stated that often teenagers had trouble in their lives with boundaries. "I tried to set limits on her behavior, as a responsible yet attractive mother. I suppose Snow White never understood that."

When asked what led to her decision to file a lawsuit, Queen Endora sighed deeply, stroking her faithful Raven perched beside her. "My attorney, Berry Blackbird, said that I had to stand up for truth, justice and the fairy tale way, and who am I to argue with that?"

Queen Endora stated that monetary damages would not be enough to repair the wound Snow White caused with her lies, adding, "I will not be happy with just taking her money and her castle. I want her to apologize to me in public, on her knees and kissing the hem of my dress. Then, of course, I will forgive her because that's the kind of person I am."

The interview was concluded when the sensitive Queen could not restrain her tears any longer. As she left the room, distraught and despairing, she promised to continue at another time with this reporter.

IN THE FAIRY TALE DISTRICT COURT
ONCE UPON A TIME DIVISION

QUEEN ENDORA:	:	
a/k/a The Evil Stepmother,	:	**CASE NO. 987654321**
	:	
Plaintiff,	:	
	:	
vs.	:	
	:	
SNOW WHITE, et al	:	
	:	
Defendants	:	
	:	

DEFENDANTS' ORIGINAL ANSWER AND COUNTERCLAIM

COMES NOW, Snow White and Poison Proof Apples, Inc., Defendants in the above entitled and numbered suit, and makes, files and presents Defendants' Original Answer and Counterclaim. In support hereof, Defendants would show the Court as follows:

Defenses

I.

Defendants Snow White and Poison Proof Apples, Inc. say that everything in Plaintiff's Original Petition is a lie.

II.

Defendant Snow White denies that she was ever a rebellious teenager.

III.

Defendant Snow White denies that she ever ran off with the huntsman.

IV.

Defendant Snow White states that she did live with seven dwarves who tried to protect her from another murder attempt.

V.

Defendant Snow White denies that she only choked on the apple.

VI.

Defendants Snow White and Poison Proof Apples, Inc. deny that the commercial is a lie.

Answer

VII.

Defendants deny each and every lie contained in Plaintiff's Original Petition and Defendants exercise their right to require Plaintiff to prove it.

Counterclaim

VIII.

Defendant Snow White states that Queen Endora did attempt to kill Snow White on at least two occasions.

WHEREFORE PREMISES CONSIDERED, Snow White and Poison Proof Apples, Inc. request that the Court set this cause for trial and that at such trial Snow White and Poison Proof Apples, Inc. receive everything to which they are justly entitled.

Respectfully Submitted,

_____

Prewitt Fox

THE QUICK BROWN FOX FIRM
711 Lazy Dog Lane
Fairy Tale Land
Telephone: 12345
Fax: 67890

ATTORNEY FOR DEFENDANTS
SNOW WHITE AND
POISON PROOF APPLES, INC.

THE FAIRYTALE TATTLER

www.tattler.tale   Day 210, Year of the Magic Carpet $1.50

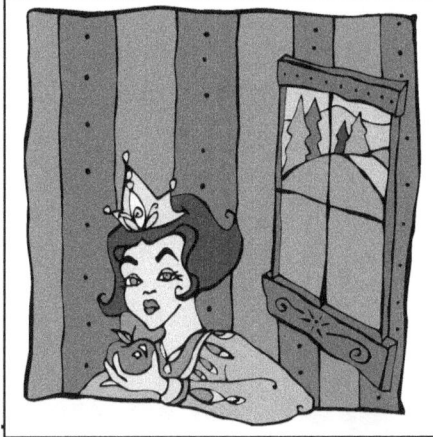

SNOW WHITE A LIAR?

Stepmother Sues Claiming Slander and Libel

CINDERELLA AND PRINCE

SEPARATION

His glass shoe fetish led to break

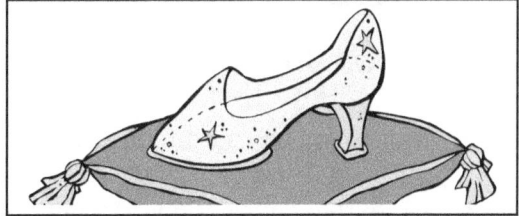

Giant Falls From Sky
Onlookers express surprise

RESCUE AT SEA:
Three men found drifting in tub

Medication Given To Irrational Numbers:
Doctors hope for a complete return to sanity.

Page 2.718281828459045235360287471352662497757247093699959574966967627724076630353547594571382178525166427427466391932003059921817413596629043572900334295260595630738132328627943490763233829880753195251019011573834187930702154089149934884157943029578320984571087364537281908365839286583928374892658961672349876123789587612347891253432800394736280972537482917878573729881029384657687365837262538496098372364758389926152437162534231421152738909746576253526172635156326879596909125863529183787987654321665748384755623761827461935503921736167283716273612662515367237271651[6]¹

A subsidiary of Endora Enterprises, Inc.   *Proud to be Fairy Tale Land's only Media Monopoly*

IN THE FAIRY TALE DISTRICT COURT
ONCE UPON A TIME DIVISION

QUEEN ENDORA **a/k/a The Evil Stepmother,**	:	
	:	**CASE NO.:987654321**
Plaintiff,	:	
	:	
vs.	:	
	:	
SNOW WHITE, et al	:	
	:	
Defendants	:	
_____	:	

<u>PLAINTIFF'S MOTION FOR SOME SORT OF JUDGMENT</u>

TO THE HONORABLE COURT:

Comes now, Queen Endora, Plaintiff in the above entitled and numbered suit and requests the Court to consider her Motion For Some Sort of Judgment pursuant to I'm Made Of Rubber, You're Made of Glue Regulations, Whatever You Say Bounces Off Me And Sticks To You §1.

Respectfully Submitted,

_____
Berry O. Blackbird

BLACKBIRD & CROW, P.C.
Attorneys at Law
909 Black Ridge Road
Fairy Tale Land

ATTORNEY FOR PLAINTIFF
QUEEN ENDORA

Telephone: 99999
FAX: 99991

IN THE FAIRY TALE DISTRICT COURT
ONCE UPON A TIME DIVISION

QUEEN ENDORA	:	
a/k/a The Evil Stepmother,	:	
	:	**CASE NO.:987654321**
Plaintiff,	:	
	:	
vs.	:	
	:	
SNOW WHITE, et al	:	
	:	
Defendants	:	
	:	

DEFENDANTS' RESPONSE TO PLAINTIFF'S MOTION FOR SOME SORT OF JUDGMENT

TO THE HONORABLE COURT:

COMES NOW, Snow White and Poison Proof Apples, Inc., Defendants in the above entitled and numbered suit and make, file and present Defendants' Response to Plaintiff's Motion for Some Sort of Judgment. Pursuant to §2 of the Rubber/Glue Regulations, Defendants respectfully state that Queen Endora is a wonderful person.

Respectfully Submitted,

_____
Prewitt Fox

THE QUICK BROWN FOX FIRM   ATTORNEY FOR DEFENDANTS
711 Lazy Dog Lane
Fairy Tale Land
Telephone: 12345
Fax: 67890

IN THE FAIRY TALE DISTRICT COURT
ONCE UPON A TIME DIVISION

QUEEN ENDORA
a/k/a The Evil Stepmother,

        Plaintiff,

vs.

SNOW WHITE, et al

        Defendants

:
:
:   **CASE NO.:987654321**
:
:
:
:
:
:
:

PLAINTIFF'S REPLY TO DEFENDANTS' RESPONSE TO PLAINTIFF'S MOTION FOR SOME SORT OF JUDGMENT

TO THE HONORABLE COURT:

Comes now, Queen Endora, Plaintiff and requests the Court to consider Plaintiff

as rubber for the attempted murderess counter accusation and as glue for the wonderful

person description.

                          Respectfully Submitted,

                          _____

                          Berry O. Blackbird

BLACKBIRD & CROW, P.C.
Attorneys at Law
909 Black Ridge Road
Fairy Tale Land

Telephone: 99999
FAX: 99991

                          ATTORNEY FOR PLAINTIFF
                          QUEEN ENDORA

IN THE FAIRY TALE DISTRICT COURT
ONCE UPON A TIME DIVISION

QUEEN ENDORA	:	
a/k/a The Evil Stepmother,	:	
	:	**CASE NO.:987654321**
Plaintiff,	:	
	:	
vs.	:	
	:	
SNOW WHITE, et al	:	
	:	
Defendants	:	
_____	:	

DEFENDANTS' ANSWER TO PLAINTIFF'S REPLY TO DEFENDANTS' RESPONSE TO PLAINTIFF'S MOTION FOR SOME SORT OF JUDGMENT

TO THE HONORABLE COURT:

COMES NOW, Snow White and Poison Proof Apples, Inc., Defendants and make, file and present Defendants' Answer to Plaintiff's Reply to Defendants' Response to Plaintiff's Motion for Some Sort of Judgment. Defendants contend that pursuant to §3 of the Rubber/Glue Regulations, Plaintiff cannot be both rubber and glue at the same time.

Respectfully Submitted,

_____

Prewitt Fox

THE QUICK BROWN FOX FIRM
711 Lazy Dog Lane
Fairy Tale Land
Telephone: 12345
Fax: 67890

ATTORNEY FOR DEFENDANTS

IN THE FAIRY TALE DISTRICT COURT
ONCE UPON A TIME DIVISION

QUEEN ENDORA **a/k/a The Evil Stepmother,**	:	
	:	
	:	**CASE NO.:987654321**
Plaintiff,	:	
	:	
vs.	:	
	:	
SNOW WHITE, et al	:	
	:	
Defendants	:	
_____	:	

PLAINTIFF'S ANGRY RETORT TO DEFENDANTS' ANSWER TO PLAINTIFF'S REPLY TO DEFENDANTS' RESPONSE TO PLAINTIFF'S <u>MOTION FOR SOME SORT OF JUDGMENT</u>

TO THE HONORABLE COURT:

    Comes now, Queen Endora, Plaintifff, in the above entitled and numbered suit

and reminds Defendant of the "Can, Too" tenet.

Respectfully Submitted,

_____

Berry O. Blackbird

BLACKBIRD & CROW, P.C.   ATTORNEY FOR PLAINTIFF
Attorneys at Law   QUEEN ENDORA
909 Black Ridge Road
Fairy Tale Land

Telephone: 99999
FAX: 99991

IN THE FAIRY TALE DISTRICT COURT
ONCE UPON A TIME DIVISION

QUEEN ENDORA **a/k/a The Evil Stepmother,**	:	
	:	
	:	**CASE NO.:987654321**
Plaintiff,	:	
	:	
vs.	:	
	:	
SNOW WHITE, et al	:	
	:	
Defendants	:	
_____	:	

ORDER
ON PLAINTIFF'S ANGRY RETORT TO DEFENDANTS' ANSWER TO PLAINTIFF'S REPLY TO DEFENDANTS' RESPONSE TO PLAINTIFF'S <u>MOTION FOR SOME SORT OF JUDGMENT</u>

On the date subscribed below came on to be considered by the Court all these ridiculous Motions and the Court, being extremely busy and thereupon annoyed by all this paperwork, hereby

ORDERS that everyone cut it out and prepare for trial. Any judgment will be rendered then and not before.

Signed this 265 day of the Year of the Magic Carpet.

_____
Thumbelina
Judge Presiding

Jack Horner's Toxin Corner, Inc.
All Poison Testing Service Center
44 Plum Drive
Fairy Tale Land

Day 254, Year of the Magic Carpet

Berry O. Blackbird, Esq.
609 Castle Ridge Rd.
Fairy Tale Land

Dear Ms. Blackbird:

I have tested the sample of fossilized apple for poisons per your request and the results are as follows:

Paint Thinner	0%
Arsenic	0%
Cyanide	0%
Poison Pen	0%
Poison Letter	0%
Broccoli	0%

Since there are many more potential poisons that could have caused Snow White's symptoms, if there is anything else you would like me to look for, please let me know.

Sincerely,

Jack Horner

JH/jh

The following is a transcript from the most popular television show in
Fairy Tale Land.

"The Opinionator"

Day 270, Year of the Magic Carpet

Young King Cole: Thank you for joining "The Opinionator", the show that clarifies

what your opinion should be on any topic. Today we'll be discussing poor Queen

Endora's lawsuit against that liar Snow White for libel and slander. Joining us today are

Goldilocks, currently President of THRT, Trespassers Have Rights Too and Rose Red,

Snow White's older sister. Good afternoon.

Goldilocks: Good Afternoon.

Rose Red: Wait a minute, Snow White isn't a liar.

Young King Cole: Oh, so we're starting right in without any niceties, are we? That's

fine, so tell me, if Snow White isn't a liar, then why was she taken to court by her own

stepmother?

Goldilocks: Obviously because royalty thinks they can get away with lying, cheating and

murder.

Young King Cole: I know. They think they are above the morals the rest of us are

expected to practice.

Rose Red: Wait a minute Cole. You're royalty, too. Are you saying that you--

Young King Cole: Now you're getting off the point, Rose. We're talking about your sister and her habitual lying. She lied to her teacher when she said the dog ate her homework. She's never even owned a dog.

Goldilocks: Typical.

Rose Red: Well, actually--

Young King Cole: She lied to Cinderella two months ago at a ball. I was there, I heard it. She said that the dress Cinderella was wearing didn't make her look fat but it really did. Sorry, Cindy, but we have pictures to prove it.

Rose Red: I hardly think--

Young King Cole: See, that's the problem right there. Not thinking. I know she's your sister, but c'mon, at least one of you should be honest here.

Rose Red: I am. Snow White is--

Young King Cole: Really? You've barely completed a sentence since you've gotten here. How is leaving out half of what you're saying honest?

Rose Red: It's not my fault if you keep--

Young King Cole: And when are people going to start taking responsibility for their own actions? All I keep hearing is that it's not my fault. Then whose fault is it?

Goldilocks: I'm disappointed in you, Rosie. I thought I knew you.

Young King Cole: Poor Queen Endora. She becomes a stepmother to Snow White and this is how she repays her, by telling everyone Queen Endora committed a crime.

Rose Red: She did.

Young King Cole: How would you know? You'd married some sort of bear prince and left home by then.

Rose Red: My husband isn't actually a bear. And I can't understand how you can assume that Queen Endora is telling the truth when everyone knows what she really is.

Goldilocks: Sounds like you'll have a lawsuit against you next.

Rose Red: I'll be sure to hire the attorney who got you off on that trespassing charge.

Young King Cole: We're not talking about Goldi here. I can't believe how often you try to change the subject. And the truth about the Queen? She marries a guy with a daughter who runs off to live with seven men.

Rose Red: They are dwarves. They're the nicest--

Young King Cole: Oh, right, that makes a big difference. What do you think, Goldi?

Goldilocks: Everything I've read about this case in the papers or heard on the radio only confirms my feelings that Snow White is guilty. If her stepmother had tried to kill her twenty years ago, why didn't she press charges then? And I'll bet she was in a coma or that sleeping death. I heard that she was in rehab for a drug problem.

Rose Red: That's not true. She was in a coma from the poisoned apple. I saw her in the glass coffin.

Young King Cole: That's easy for you to say.

Rose Red: We have pictures.

Young King Cole: Oh, like pictures can't be faked.

Rose Red: Other people came by and saw her.

Young King Cole: Yeah, and all the little forest creatures, too.

Rose Red: This is ridiculous. Why did you invite me here if all you're going to do is--

Young King Cole: You knew we were going to ask tough questions about your sister.

Rose Red: Yes, but I expected to be able to--

Goldilocks: Royalty can be such sore losers.

Rose Red: That does it. I don't have to take this. I don't know why I even bothered coming on this show since Endora owns it. I'm leaving.

Young King Cole: You can't leave. Guests don't leave our show in the middle of the interview. Hey, get back here. We're not done with the segment. You'll be sorry. We'll be right back after these commercial messages…Well, put some on!

909 Black Ridge Road
Fairy Tale Land
Telephone: 99999
Fax: 99991

BLACKBIRD & CROW, P.C.
Smart Lawyers who look fantastic in black

Internet: blackbird&crow@darkcolors.com

Day 271, Year of the Magic Carpet

Prewitt Fox, Esq.
The Quick Brown Fox Firm
711 Lazy Dog Lane

BY PIGEON POST

    RE: Case No. 987654321; Queen Endora v. Snow White, *et al*

Dear Mr. Fox:

Although Queen Endora is devastated by the destruction of her reputation by your clients, she has generously authorized me to settle the case upon the following terms:

(A)   Snow White will prepare a Public Apology, which she will read aloud on the Fairy Tale Evening News;

(B)   The Public Apology will contain an It's All My Fault Clause;

(C)   Poison Proof Apples, Inc. will turn over all its inventory to Queen Endora so she can turn it into applesauce; and

(D)   Snow White will give up her Fairy Tale Princess status and work as Queen Endora's ladies maid.

If your clients find the proposed settlement agreeable, which of course they should if they have any common sense, please signify by endorsing the bottom of this letter on the designated line and return it to me by the close of business. Otherwise, the offer will be withdrawn forever.

In the event that you have any questions you may contact me at my convenience.

Very truly yours,

Berry O. Blackbird

BOB/jay

cc: Queen Endora

_____

Designated Line

THE QUICK BROWN FOX FIRM

711 Lazy Dog Lane
Fairy Tale Land
quickbrownfox@jumpsoverdog.net
greyhound@driving2us.net

Prewitt Fox, Esq.   Grey Hound, Esq.

Telephone: 12345   Fax: 67890

Day 272, Year of the Magic Carpet

Berry O. Blackbird, Esq.
Blackbird & Crow, P.C.
909 Black Ridge Road
Fairy Tale Land

Dear Ms. Blackbird:

With regard to your offer of settlement, my clients Snow White and Poison Proof Apples, Inc. have authorized me to give this as their reply:

Hahahahah!

See you in court,

Prewitt Fox

PF/pf

cc: Snow White
         Poison Proof Apples, Inc.

LIVE FROM THE COURTHOUSE
Day 288
Red Riding Hood Reporting

"Jacques, don't jiggle the camera. You're making me look like I'm in an earthquake. How's my hair? Anything stuck in my teeth? I'm lucky the producer gave me another chance to get on the air after you didn't tell me about the broccoli last week. Ready? Are we on? Ten seconds?" Red Riding Hood smoothed her hair, adjusted her hood and smiled.

"This is Red Riding Hood, reporting live for Channel 1 from the courthouse. We're here waiting for Snow White to arrive for the first day of her trial for libel brought against her by the beautiful Queen Endora ---cut, cut. I can't believe this. Jacques, I'm over here. Oh. Why didn't you tell me it was Snow White? You've just ruined perfectly good footage by not telling me. Ready? Let's try this again. This is Red Riding Hood reporting live from the courthouse. We're here to keep you up to date on Snow White's trial for libel, brought by the much-maligned Queen Endora. The word on the street is that it doesn't look good for Snow White. We have here a man who saw Snow White arriving a short time ago. And what is your name?"

"Jack Sprat."

"Mr. Sprat, tell us your impressions of how the trial is affecting Snow White."

"She looks like she's eating too many carbohydrates and getting too much protein from fat. I recommend a lean diet, with plenty of grains, beans, legumes, fruits and raw vegetables. Most people assume this will cause a lot of gas, but this only lasts a few weeks. Maybe she'd better wait until the trial is over."

"Thank you, Mr. Sprat. How about you ma'am? What do you think?"

"I'm Mrs. Sprat. I don't agree with my husband at all. I think she's looking rather thin, poor thing. Her life has been so difficult lately. She'd look a lot healthier more fleshed out so she should add fats to her diet. I recommend any food that uses lots of butter and sugar. The more the better."

"Thank you, Mrs. Sprat. Can't believe we're talking about diets here. Let's move on to another bystander. What's your name and what do you think of Snow White?"

"My name is Mistress Mary, and I am not trying to be contrary, but I think Snow White is not a liar. It's Queen Endora who wouldn't recognize the truth if it were wearing a nametag. I think the public should join in this lawsuit-"

"And those are the feelings of the public here at the courthouse on the first day of Snow White's trial. The verdict is that Snow White is a liar. Back to the studio." Red Riding Hood stopped smiling, took off her hood, and fluffed up her hair.

"Okay, Jacques, just use Mistress Mary's comments but make sure to take out the word 'not'. Remember who owns the station. I'm off to breakfast with Jack Horner. I'm breaking up with him because all he talks about is pie."

OLD WOMAN WHO LIVES IN SHOE: MEAN
TO HER CHILDREN
By
Willie Ann Winkie

This reporter has just discovered that Mrs. Lace, retired royal nanny, had been charged with being unreasonably mean to her children for spanking them when they misbehaved and feeding them bread without any broth.

Her neighbor, an old woman who was sitting in a large basket and holding a broom, remarked, "I don't have any children, but if I did, I wouldn't spank them. If they needed discipline, I'd give them positive reinforcement like gold stickers for good behavior."

When questioned about being charged with being mean to her poor children, Mrs. Lace retorted, "You try having all them children in that little bitty shoe we live in. They're always underfoot and fighting with each other and they never pick up after themselves. I'm not their maid! I tried that reward system once. Did those hooligans care about gold stickers and charts? Not them.

"Once I started using negative reinforcement you'd be surprised at how quickly they shaped up. And then the judge dismissed the charges and gave me an honorary plaque for Mother of the Year. Hector, put your sister down! No, I didn't mean drop her out the window. Polly, we don't want cinders thrown on us. Mary, her tape recorder is not a sczzneidng…"

This reporter requests hazard pay and reimbursement for new equipment.

DELETED SCENE:

MS. BLACKBIRD: The Plaintiff calls Vanessa Vulture to the stand.

(The Witness is sworn in)

MS. BLACKBIRD: State your name for the record.

THE WITNESS: Vanessa Vulture.

MS. BLACKBIRD: Are you married?

V. VULTURE: Was. Husband died two years ago. Ate meat that was too fresh.

MS. BLACKBIRD: What is your occupation?

V. VULTURE: Clean up environment.

MS. BLACKBIRD: How do you do that?

V. VULTURE: Eat remains of dead, rotting things so other creatures can enjoy

scenery.

MS. BLACKBIRD: Do you remember a night about twenty years ago?

V.VULTURE: Might.

MS. BLACKBIRD: This night it was storming and some dwarves were chasing

an old peddler woman who fell off a cliff?

V. VULTURE: Humans. Don't get them often.

MS. BLACKBIRD: So you do remember that one –er, dish?

V. VULTURE: Yes. Old woman. Chased by dwarves. Fell off cliff. We cleaned

up.

MS. BLACKBIRD: Thank you Vanessa. You've been very helpful.

THE COURT: Your turn, Mr. Fox.

MR. FOX: Mrs. Vulture. What did you have for dinner yesterday?

V. VULTURE: Something dead.

MR. FOX: Yes, but what?

V. VULTURE: Don't know.

MR. FOX: What did you have to eat the day before yesterday.

V. VULTURE: Something dead.

MR. FOX: Yes. Of course. But what was it?

V. VULTURE: Don't know.

MR. FOX: Let me get this straight. You don't remember what you ate yesterday or the day before yesterday, but you remember a night twenty years ago and some peddler woman?

V. VULTURE: Sorry. Must go. New roadkill to clean up. (Witness flies off witness stand and out the window.)

MR. FOX: I must protest. The Defense isn't finished with this witness.

MS. BLACKBIRD: I was finished.

THE COURT: Well, if we find her again before the trial is over, we'll put her back on the stand. In the meantime, Ms. Blackbird, please call your next witness.

About the Vulture
By
Willie Ann Winkie

Vultures don't need Karate for self-defense because they just open their beaks and vomit. Georgie Porgie learned this the hard way and he is suing Vanessa Vulture for assault.

According to Georgie Porgie, he was practicing throwing rocks when one accidentally hit Vanessa Vulture while she was working. Ms. Vulture thought she was under attack and retaliated in the usual vulture manner by vomiting on Georgie Porgie.

"It was the worst experience of my life," Georgie said. Doctors are not sure if the odor from the vomit will ever go away. "This sure cramps my love life. Every time I get close to a girl, the smell is so strong that it brings tears to her eyes." Georgie hasn't been able to be one of the guys, either. "They tend to beat me up because of the smell, so I run away when I see them," he admitted sadly.

The Organization For Vulture Awareness (OFVA) has criticized Georgie for his lawsuit. They claim the publicity surrounding the lawsuit has hurt their attempt at marketing "The Ultimate Germ Killer" whose main ingredient is vulture urine. Even though no manufacturer has been willing to produce the product yet, vultures hope for the success of their pee. "This is a natural product, environmentally safe and strong enough to kill all bacteria we encounter on the job," enthused Vic Vulture, president of OPEV. "I can't imagine why it wouldn't sell."

THE FAIRY TALE TATTLER

www.tattler.tale   Day 289, Year of the Magic Carpet $1.50

HUNTSMAN MISSING:

Snow White Lost Most Important Witness

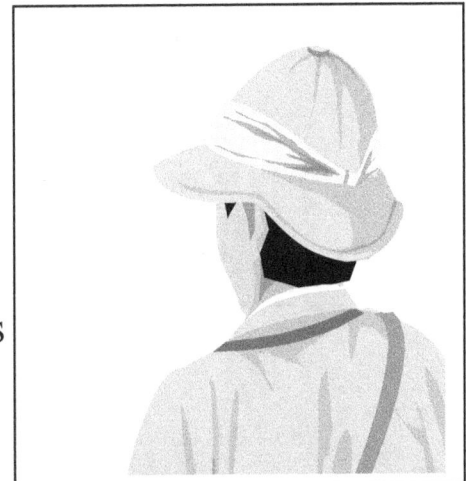

See Related Story:
Snow White's Apple Aversion

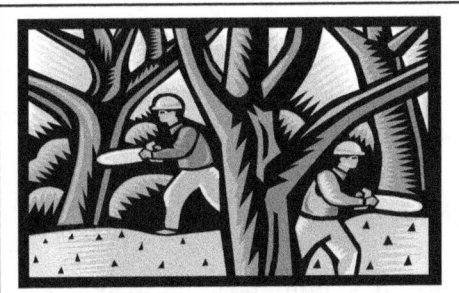

PUPPET BECOMES
REAL BOY:

Forest Rangers Alarmed At
Implications For Environment

Giant Killer Jack Claims Self Defense

English and Psychology Majors Stunned:
Gerunds discovered to have split personalities.

As Nouns: pg 10   As Verbs: pg 12

IN THE FAIRY TALE DISTRICT COURT
ONCE UPON A TIME DIVISION

QUEEN ENDORA	:	
a/k/a The Evil Stepmother,	:	
	:	**CASE NO.:987654321**
Plaintiff,	:	
	:	
vs.	:	
	:	
SNOW WHITE, et al	:	
	:	
Defendant	:	
_____	:	

FINAL JUDGMENT

On this day came on to be heard the above referenced cause and counterclaim. During the course of the proceedings Plaintiff Queen Endora occasioned to confess that she did attempt to poison Snow White, thus Snow White is not guilty of slander and libel. Accordingly, it is hereby

ORDERED that Plaintiff's suit is forthwith DISMISSED. It is further

ORDERED that Defendants' counterclaim is upheld. It is further

ORDERED that Queen Endora a/k/a the Evil Stepmother be remanded for the remainder of her life without possibility of parole to the place which is reserved as the severest punishment and torture for the most hardened criminals who have succumbed to the dark side, namely the Perpetually Perky Place.

Signed this _____ day, Year of the Magic Carpet.

_____
Thumbelina
Judge Presiding

THE FAIRY GODMOTHER INSTITUTE
1970 Bibbity Way
Fairy Tale Land

Invoice Submitted To:

Snow White
Castle on the Hill
Fairy Tale Land

Invoice No. 1213141516
DUE UPON RECEIPT

Day 289, Year of the Magic Carpet

RE: The Evil Stepmother v. Snow White

Professional Services:

	HR/Rate	AMT
Initial Telephone call received from Client	0.10 40.00/hr	35.00
Trip to Video Store	0.20 40.00/hr	70.00
Court Appearance w/Client 3.00	150/hr	450.00
PROFESSIONAL SERVICES RENDERED:		655.00

Additional Charges:

Reimbursement for Tape and DVD	50.00
Parking at Courthouse	3.00
Dry Cleaning for stains on uniform From popcorn	6.00
ADDITIONAL CHARGES:	59.00
TOTAL AMOUNT OF THIS BILL:	**714.00**

The Fairy Godmother Institute thanks you for your prompt payment. If no payment is received within 30 days, all wishes granted to client will be rescinded.

THE FAIRYTALE TATTLER

www.tattler.tale   Day 290, Year of the Magic Carpet $1.50

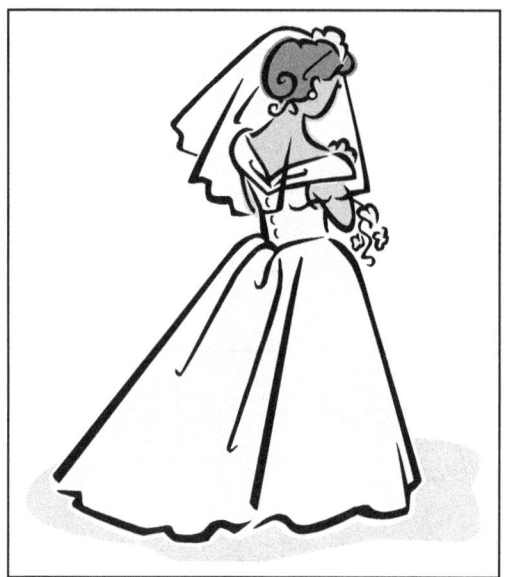

SNOW WHITE

INNOCENT

WILL ATTEND DAUGHTER'S WEDDING

SEVEN SISTERS

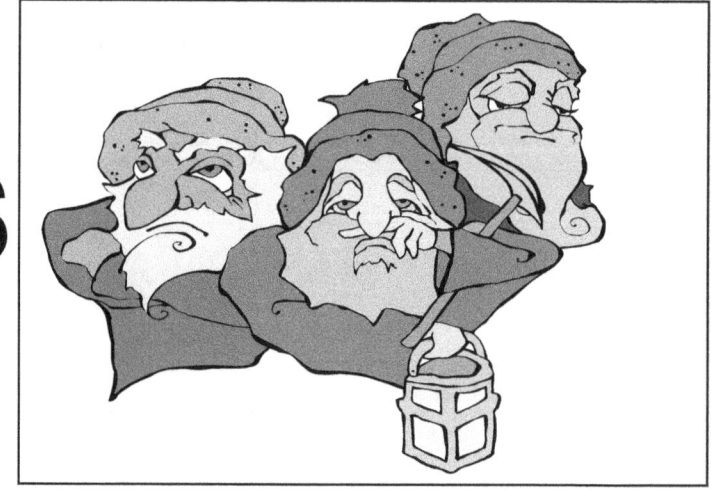

WAKE DWARVES FROM SPELL WITH TRUE LOVE'S KISS: Surprise!

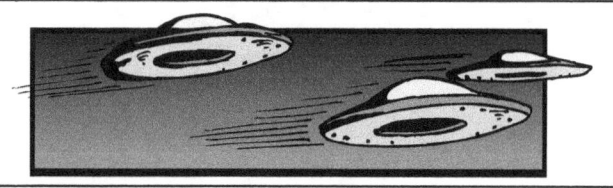

Huntsman Found:
I WAS KIDNAPPED BY ALIENS

Tortoise Wins Race; Rabbits Cry Foul.

Spider Spout Race Rained Out

**Phoenetists in Uproar:
Silent Letters Insist On Equal Pronunciation**

CRIMINAL ACTIVITY

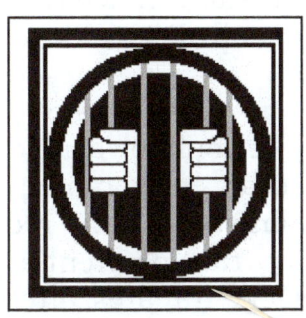

Episodes based on Real Events.
A New Episode Guaranteed When Another Crime Is Committed.

Season Premiere Tonight 8 p.m.

Criminal Activity brings you the true story of the downfall of Queen Endora, a/k/a The Evil Stepmother.

ONLY ON CHANNEL ONE
(Under New Ownership)
Number 1 because it's the only station in Fairy Tale Land

Sponsored by
Poison Proof Apples, Inc.

"I'VE BEEN FRAMED!"
by
Willie Ann Winkie-Horner

"I really have," insisted the Evil Stepmother, at an exclusive interview with this reporter at the convicted Queen's current and lifetime residence, the dreaded Perpetually Perky Place. "I've been here six months and it feels like six lifetimes."

Perpetually Perky Place could be considered paradise, but the truly evil cannot be comfortable in an environment that only allows goodness. Founded by the eternally optimistic girl who reduced an entire cold hearted town to sappy sentimentality, this penitentiary has soothing music and aromatherapy round the clock. Inmates attend daily sing-alongs, yoga, acupuncture, painting class (only pastel colors allowed) and comedy therapy. They are all required to read books and watch movies or television shows with a happy ending or a moral to the story. Even the food is cheerful; no plate leaves the kitchen without the food forming a smiley face.

The Queen's eyes were red and puffy from crying. "I'm sick of everyone being so kind and I hate singing." This reporter gave the Evil Stepmother a tissue to wipe the glob of snot hanging from her nose.

The Evil Stepmother had no idea why Snow White would hate her so much to frame her. "With the lawsuit, I tried to teach her that she couldn't get away with lying about me, but I suppose Snow White never understood that."

When asked if she regretted deciding to sue Snow White, the Evil Stepmother said that her only regret was not finishing her off with that Poisoned Apple. Queen Endora added, "Nothing will make up for this torture. Well, maybe if I can kill her. Then, of course, I will forgive her because that's the kind of person I am."

"And the worst thing of all is that they call me Dora here! Every time I correct them they smile. Why can't I be sent into solitary? Thrown into a dungeon? I like chains. I want to be tortured properly. Why don't we have gruel? I'm tired of comfort food."

As Dora ended the interview, distraught and despairing, this reporter decided not to interview her again.

A Few Legal Definitions: What They Really Mean

1. **A/K/A** – short for also known as, but sounds cooler.

2. **Court** – where the Plaintiff and Defendant take their problem. The Judge is also referred to as "the Court" because he or she decides who is right.

3. **Defendant** – the person who'd better have a good explanation for what someone said they did.

4. **et al** – means that there are more people on the list but it takes too much time to write all of them.

5. **Go hence without day** – lawyers like to use this phrase because it sounds important, but it only means to do it today, now, immediately if not sooner, what's taking you so long, should have been done yesterday.

6. **Libel and Slander** – when someone says something so bad about someone to so many people that it ruins his or her life. This is way beyond just talking bad about someone behind her back, which isn't very nice. Libel is written and slander is spoken.

7. **Original Petition** – the first paper that the Plaintiff writes that complains about the Defendant.

8. **Plaintiff** – the person who is complaining about something someone else did.

9. **WHEREFORE PREMISES CONSIDERED** – this phrase is often the opening line of the last paragraph on legal papers. Secretaries write it in capital letters because they are so happy the typing is almost done.

www.ingramcontent.com/pod-product-compliance
Lightning Source LLC
Chambersburg PA
CBHW080723190526
45169CB00006B/2496